202
CHECKMATES
for Children

ABOUT THE AUTHORS

FRED WILSON

Fred Wilson is among the finest chess teachers and authors. He and Bruce Alberston are the authors of *303 Tricky Chess Tactics* and *303 Tricky Checkmates* for Cardoza Publishing, as well as three other books: *A Picture History of Chess, 101 Questions on How to Play Chess*, and *202 Surprising Mate*s (also with Alberston). He has also edited *Classical Chess Matches: 1907-1913*, and *Lesser-Known Chess Masterpieces: 1906-1915*. Wilson is the owner of Fred Wilson Chess Books in New York City.

BRUCE ALBERSTON

Bruce Alberston is a well-known chess trainer and teacher in the New York City area. He has written and narrated the best-selling CD-ROM, *Quick Kills on the Chessboard*, and collaborated with Fred Wilson on *202 Surprising Mates, 303 Tricky Chess Tactics* and *303 Tricky Checkmates*. Alberston has also done significant research and analysis for Bruce Pandolfini who has written 17 books for Simon & Schuster.

202
CHECKMATES
for Children

Fred Wilson & Bruce Alberston

CARDOZA PUBLISHING

Cardoza Publishing is the foremost gaming publisher in the world, with a library of over 100 up-to-date and easy-to-read books and strategies. These authoritative works are written by the top experts in their fields and, with more than 7,500,000 books in print, represent the best-selling and most popular gaming books anywhere.

FIRST EDITION

Library of Congress Catalog Card No: 2004101408
ISBN: 1-58042-141-5

Visit our web site (www.cardozapub.com)
or write us for a full list of books and computer strategies.

CARDOZA PUBLISHING
P.O. Box 1500, Cooper Station, New York, NY 10276
Phone (800)577-WINS
email: cardozapub@aol.com
www.cardozapub.com

A special thanks to Jill, Anca, Michele, Riley, Rita and Marianna for their endless patience and support.

TABLE OF CONTENTS

INTRODUCTION

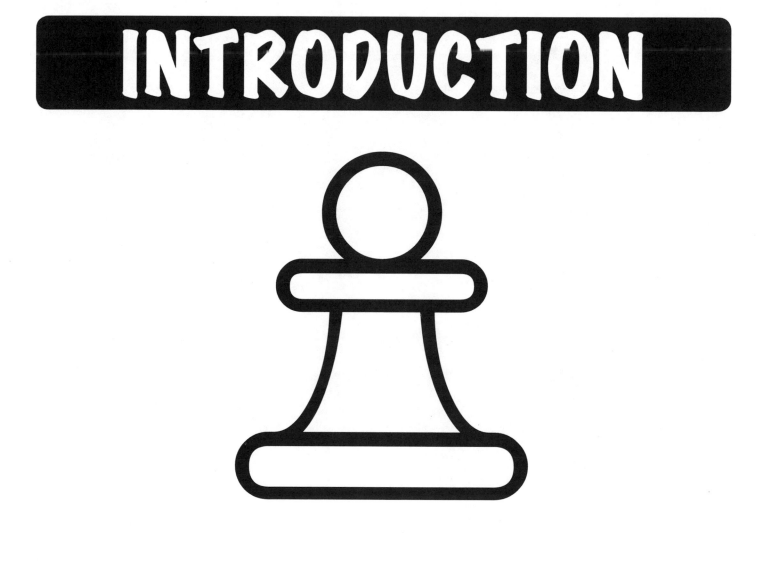

INTRODUCTION

This is your chess workbook. Here you will practice finding checkmates in one or two moves, which might happen in your own games. It is very important to practice a lot if you want to become a great chess player. Finding forced checkmates from chess diagrams is one of the best ways to get that practice. Try to solve all the checkmate diagrams in this book. Even if you don't see the answer right away, keep trying for a while.

We assume you know how to name the squares and can read a couple of moves in chess notation. If you can't find the answer, all the solutions are given at the end of the book in algebraic chess notation and with diagrams. The only two symbols that may be new to you are "**+**," which means **check** and "**#**," which is **checkmate**. However, if you want to review chess notation, see the key on page 17.

The first one hundred chess diagrams in this book show White to move, and mate in one move. These should not be too difficult because all you have to do is find the right check!

Try to solve the position below:

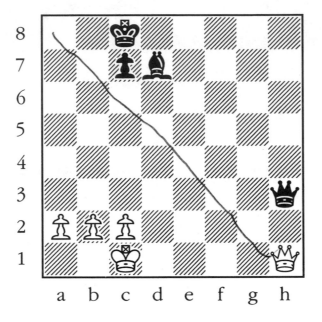

Well, did you find it? If not, here's a hint: look for a "long move." Do you see it now? Right! The queen moves to the a8 square for checkmate. The mating move in chess notation is **1. Qa8#**. We would prefer that you write your answers down either under each diagram or on a separate sheet of paper.

However, if you are still unsure how to write correct chess notation, you may write your answers for the one-move checkmates by drawing an arrow on the diagram from the checkmating piece to the square you are moving it to. Please look at the next diagram to see how this is done.

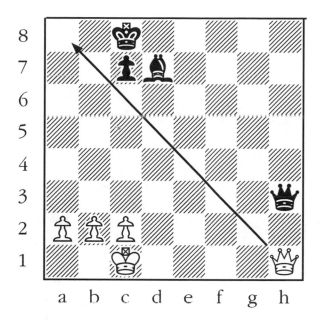

The checkmates in two moves are harder to find and will require more work. We suggest you first look for strong checks, which force the king to a square where it can be checkmated, or clever "quiet" moves, which can also threaten an unstoppable checkmate. Also, look for a big sacrifice, especially of a queen or a rook, which can break through the Black king's defenses.

We hope by the time you try to solve the checkmates in two moves, you will be able to write down the answers in chess notation. After all, it would certainly look clumsy to have three different arrows on the same diagram!

After solving the checkmates in one move, you will go on to the next 102 diagrams. In these diagrams, you will have to solve the checkmate in two moves, not one, but it is still White to move.

These checkmates are a bit trickier since they involve some extra work, but once you get going and you know what to look for, you'll be amazed at how simple it can be!

Now look at the diagram below and see if you can find a checkmate for White in two moves:

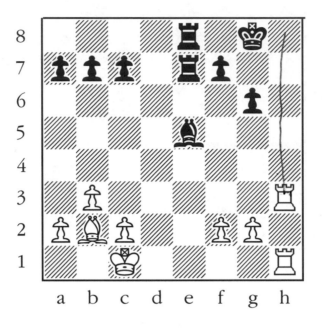

If you look at this position carefully, you will see that White has doubled rooks on the open h-file. Do you see the mate yet? If not, ask yourself, "How many times is White really attacking the square h8?" That's right! The correct solution is: **1. Rh8+ Bxh8 2. Rxh8#**.

We know it can be hard to see ahead two moves, but we also know that you would not want to miss the chance to see such a nice checkmate in one of your games. If you practice finding the checkmates in this workbook many times, you will also create many more checkmates when you play, and will become a much stronger player.

Good luck and have fun!

CHESS NOTATION

KEY FOR CHESS NOTATION

This section is to get you more familiar with chess notation so the answers in the back of the book don't look like gobbledy-gook. We're going to run through a short game played by one of the authors. Try to follow the score and the notation as the moves are presented. We'll give a diagram after several moves so you can check yourself. Refer to the key below for any help with notation.

K = King
Q = Queen
R = Rook
B = Bishop
N = Knight
+ = check
 # = checkmate
0-0 = castles kingside
0-0-0 = castles queenside
x = a capture.

Remember, when indicating a capture, you write the square you are making the capture on, rather than the piece you are capturing. We no longer use the symbol P for pawn. A pawn move is indicated by a **lower-case letter**, which identifies the file of the moving pawn.

Opening: Four Knights Game

Bruce Alberston versus Amateur (Pa., 1980)

1. e4		e5
2. Nf3		Nc6
3. Nc3		Nf6
4. Bb5		Bb4

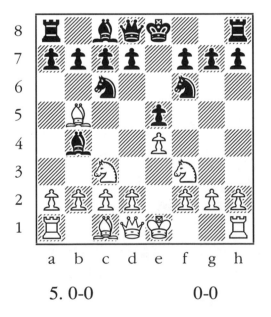

5. 0-0   0-0

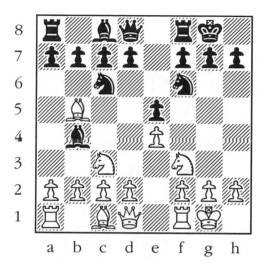

Both sides have castled their kings on the kingside. Add another zero, 0-0-0, and that means queenside castling. That didn't happen and it's not going to. You can only castle once per game.

6. d3	d6
7. Bg5	Bg4
8. Nd5	Nd4

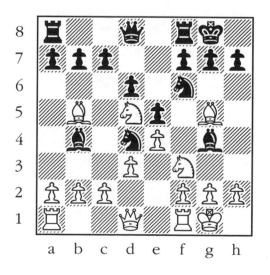

So far the play has been symmetrical. Now we get our first set of captures.

19

9. Nxb4   Nxb5

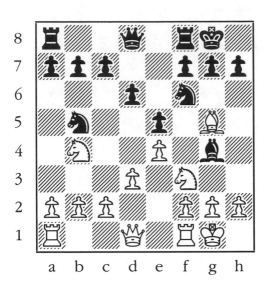

The knights have captured the bishops.

10. Nd5   Nd4

11. Qd2   Bxf3

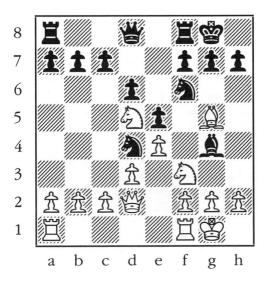

The knights have returned to their central posts and for a brief moment we get a break in the symmetry.

12. Bxf6	Qd7
13. Qg5	Qg4

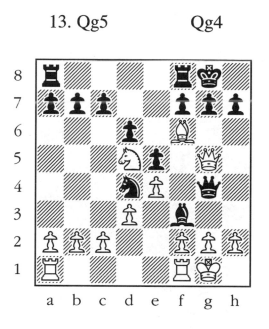

The symmetry has been restored as both sides move closer to the opposing kings and threaten to give checkmate. The problem with copying the other guy's moves is that you can't copy a check! You have to stop what you're doing and save your king. That's what happens next. In fact, it's a chess problem. White to mate in two moves.

14. Ne7+	Kh8

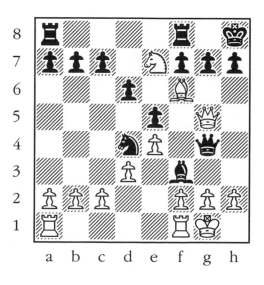

White has given a knight check. Black had only one response to save his king. He had to move into the corner. Now it's down to checkmate in one move. Do you see it?

15. Bxg7#　　　　1-0

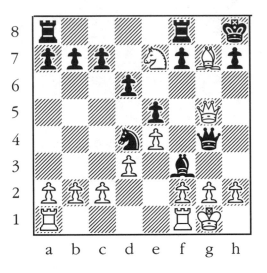

Checkmate by the bishop. The 1-0 means that White wins (0-1 means that Black wins). As you know, the symbol for checkmate is the pound sign (#).

Now that we've reviewed chess notation, it's time to try our hand at some checkmates!

THE CHECKMATES

CHECKMATE IN ONE MOVE

Remember, the first 100 positions—diagram numbers 1-100—are always White to play and checkmate in one move. The next 102 positions, diagram numbers 101-202, are always White to play and checkmate in two moves. We recommend you play through this workbook as many times as necessary until you find it easy to solve all the checkmates. The more often you practice, the easier it gets.

1.

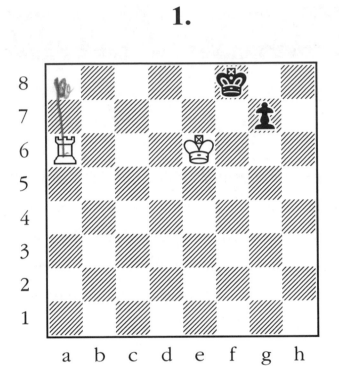

2.

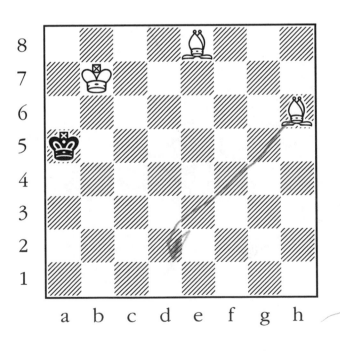

3.

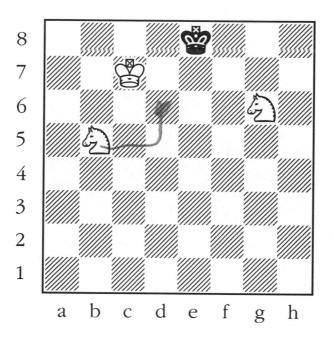

4.

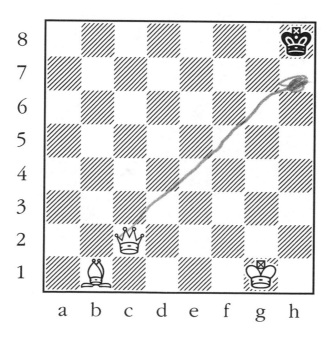

5.

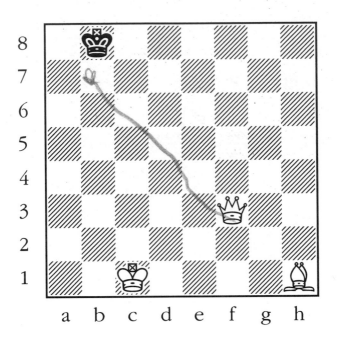

6.

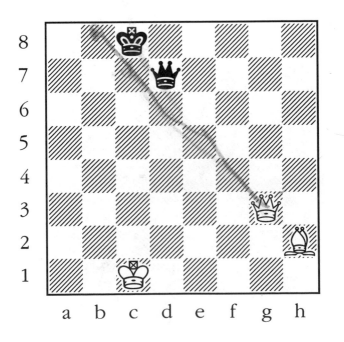

7.

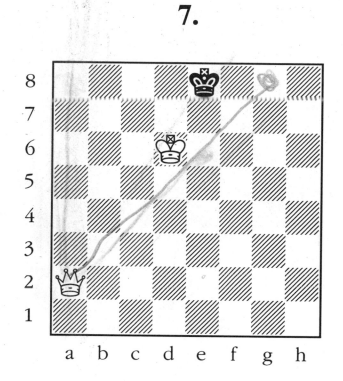

8.

9.

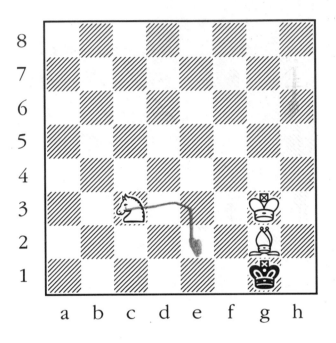

10.

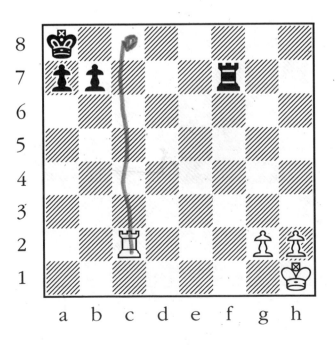

11.

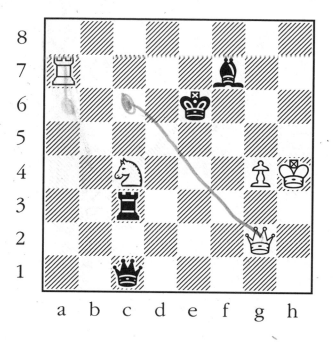

12.

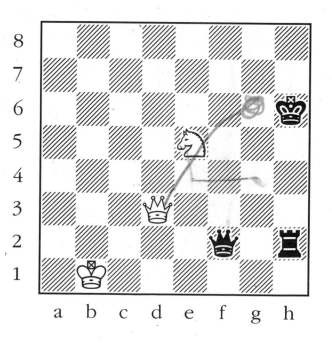

13.

14.

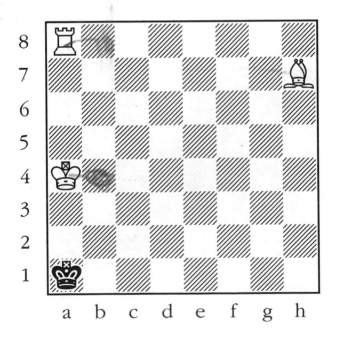

15.

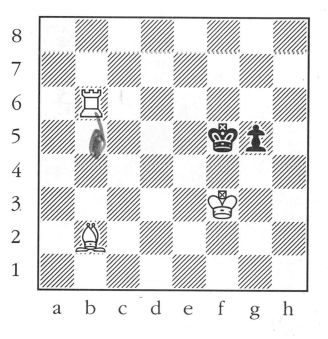

16.

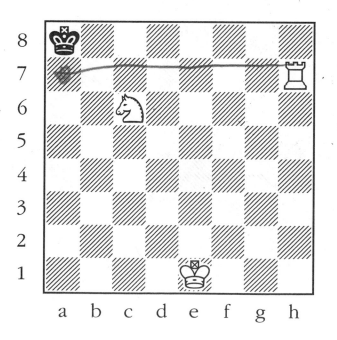

17.

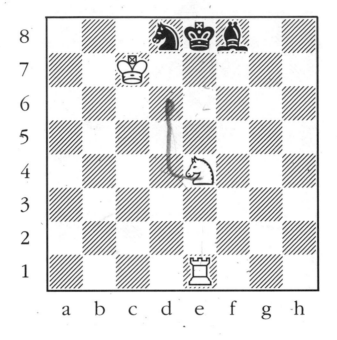

18.

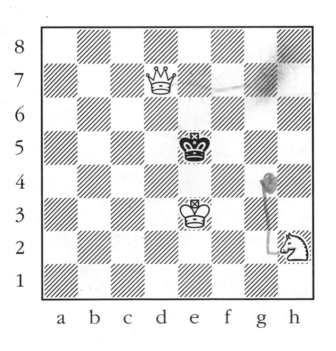

19.

20.

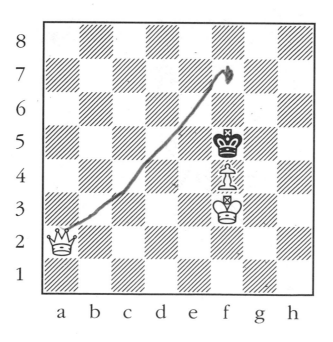

21.

22.

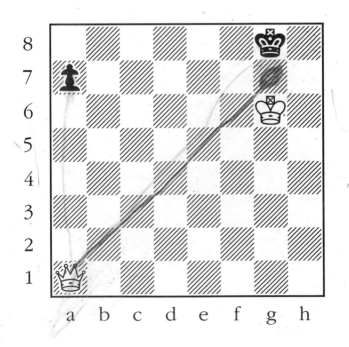

23.

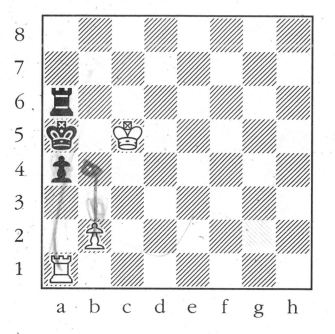

24.

25.

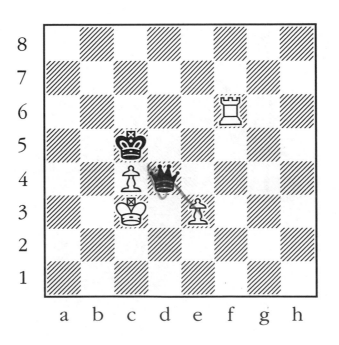

26.

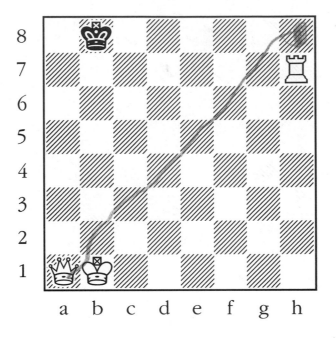

27.

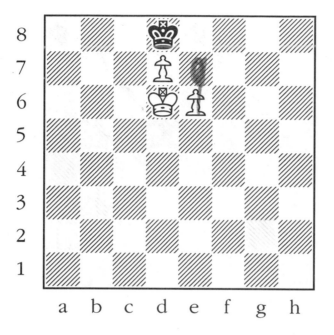

28.

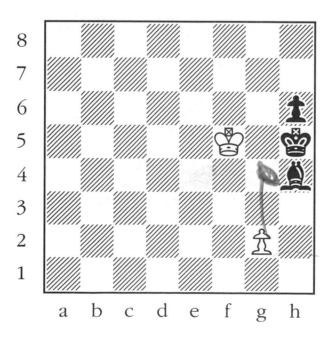

29.

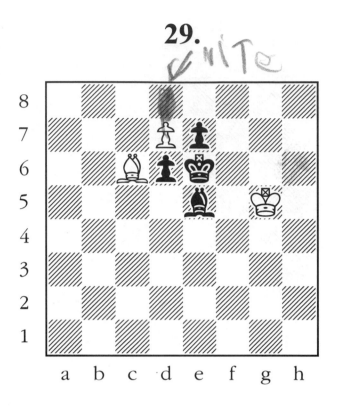

30.

31.

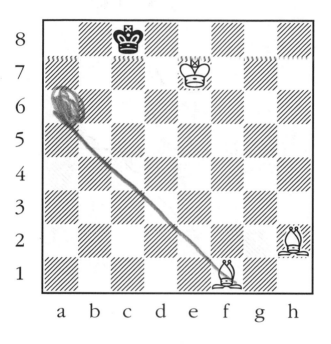

32.

33.

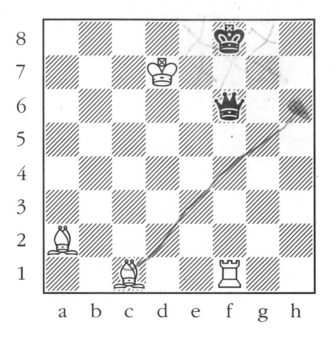

34.

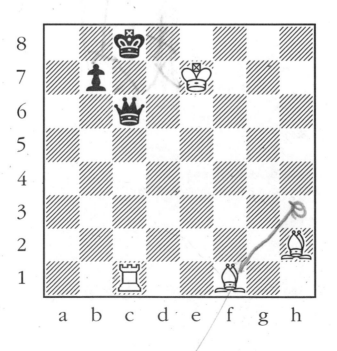

35.

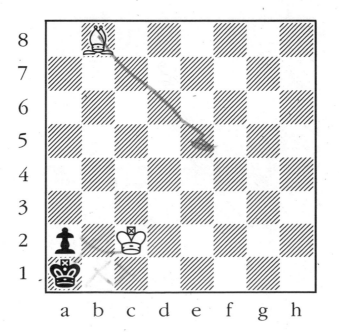

36.

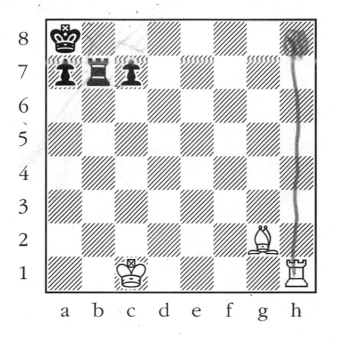

37.

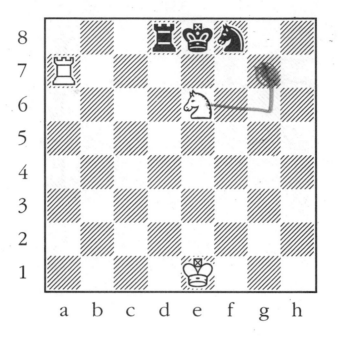

38.

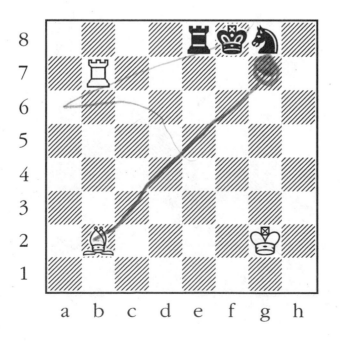

39.

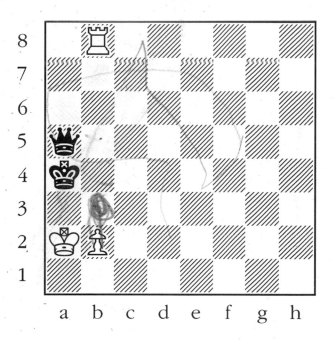

40.

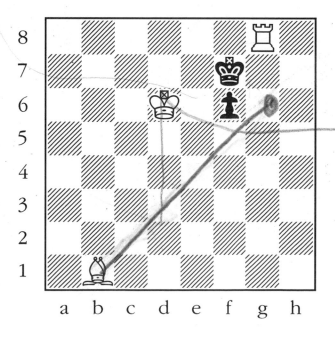

41.

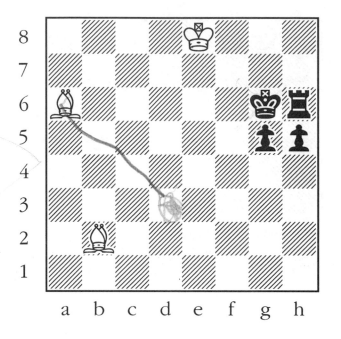

42.

43.

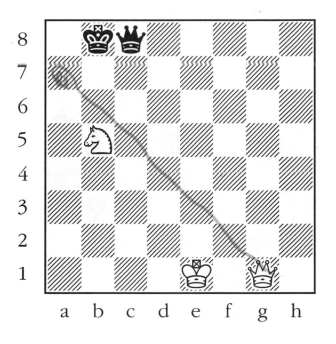

44.

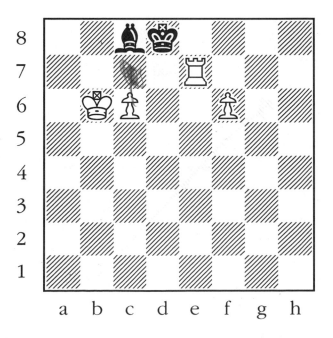

45.

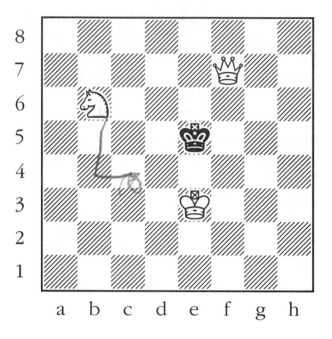

46.

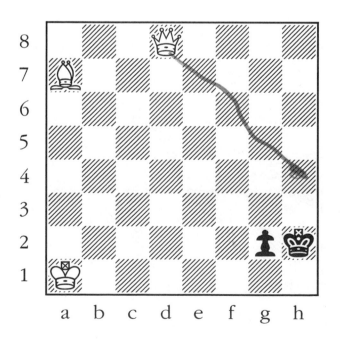

47.

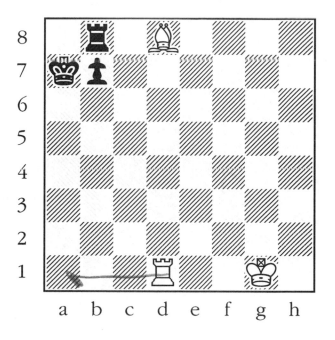

48.

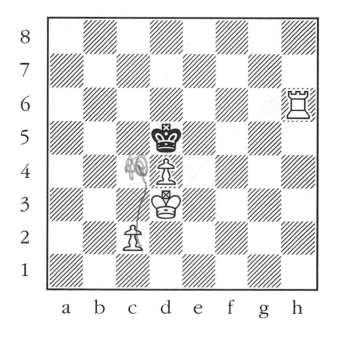

49.

50.

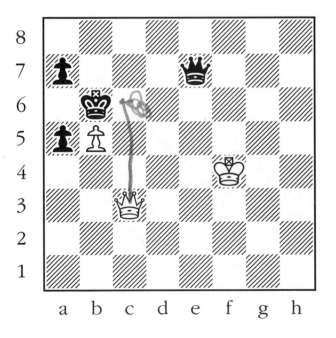

51.

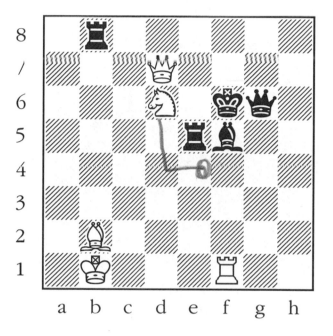

52.

53.

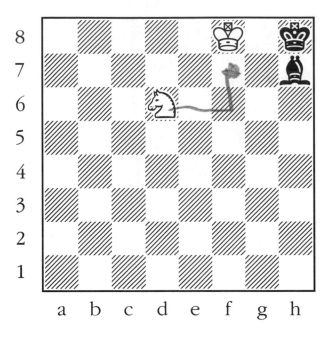

54.

55.

56.

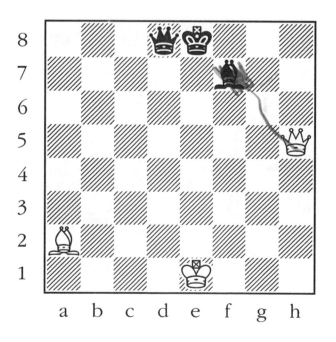

57.

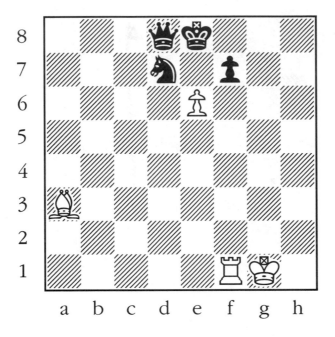

58.

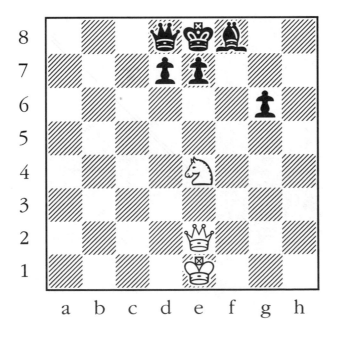

59.

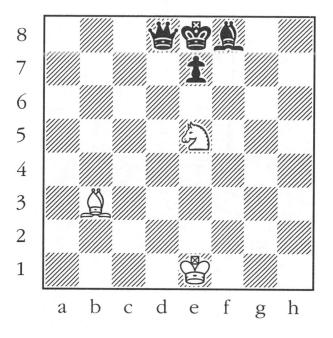

60.

61.

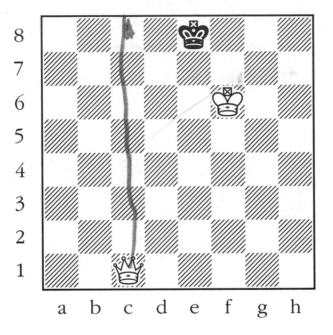

62.

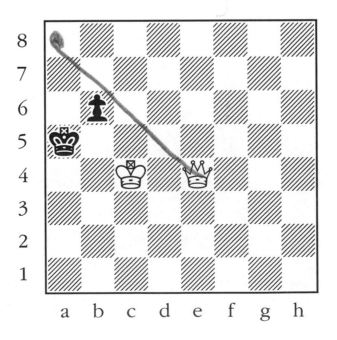

63.

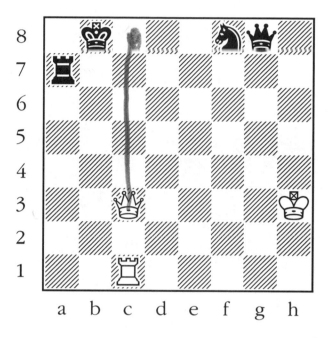

64.

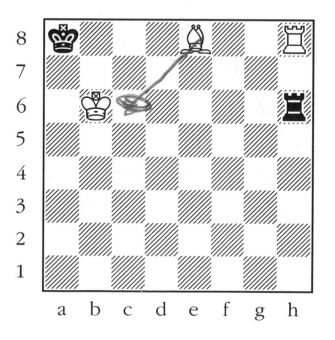

65.

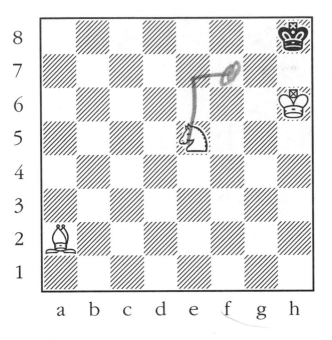

66.

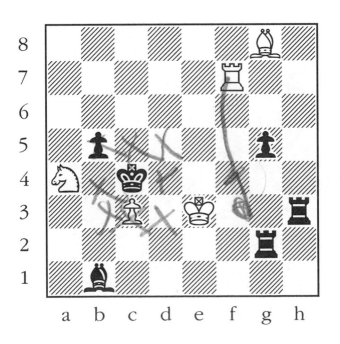

67.

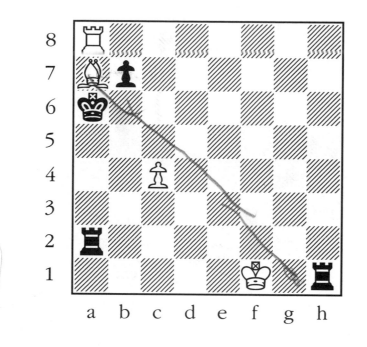

68.

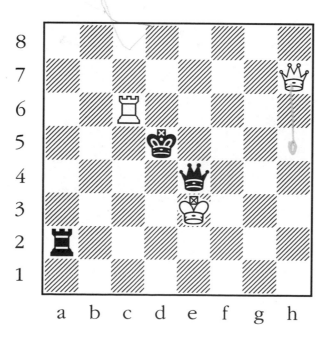

69.

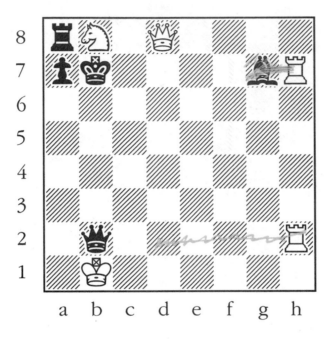

70.

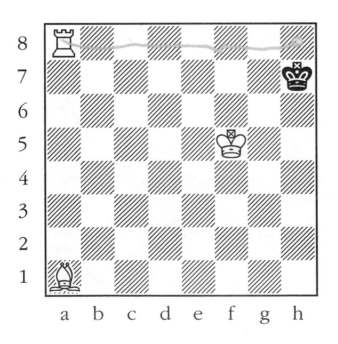

71.

72.

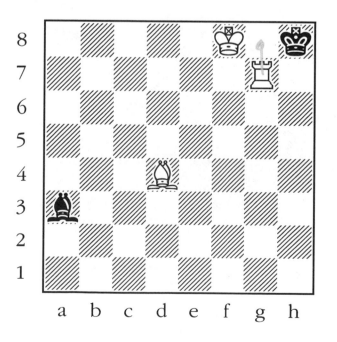

73.

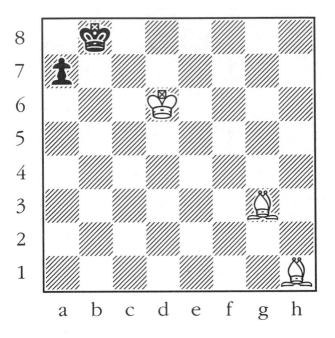

74.

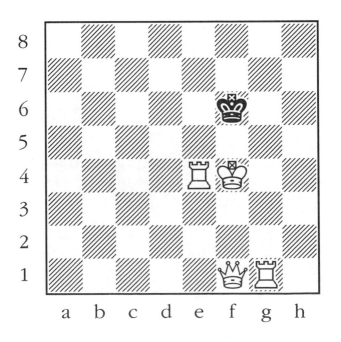

75.

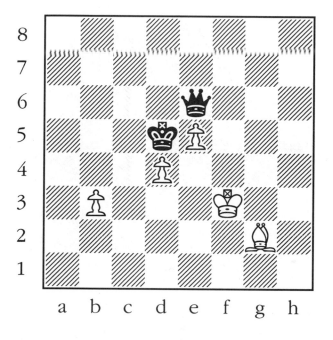

76.

77.

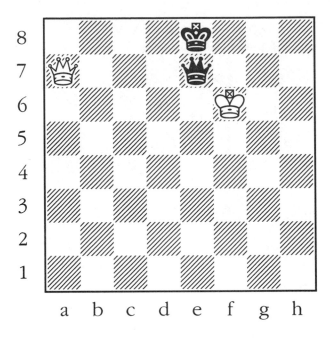

78.

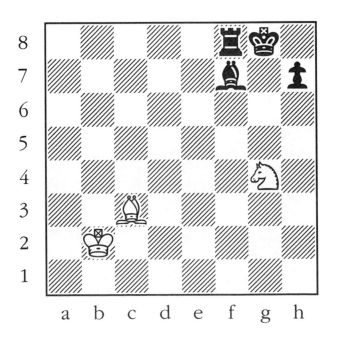

79.

80.

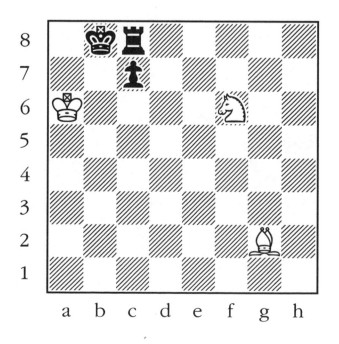

81.

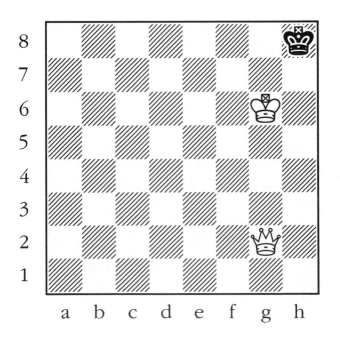

82.

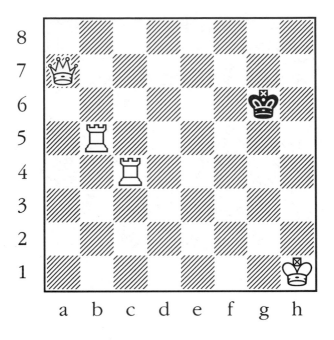

83.

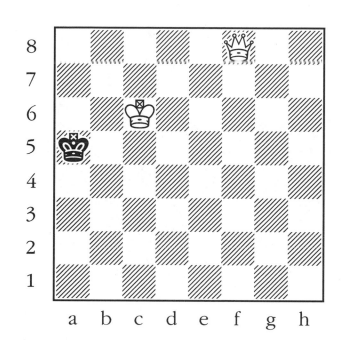

84.

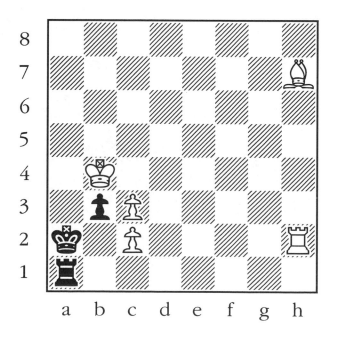

85.

86.

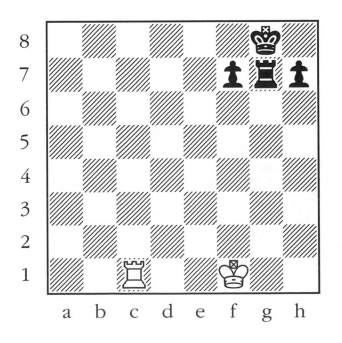

87.

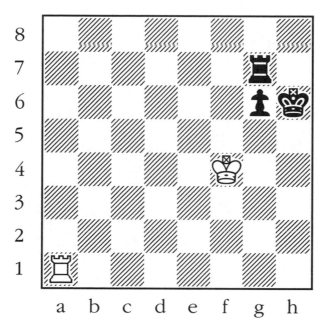

88.

89.

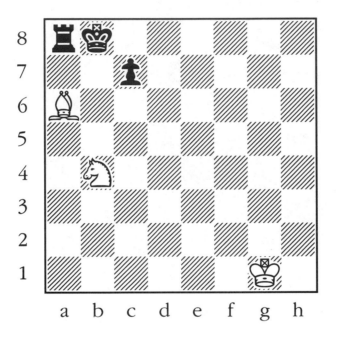

90.

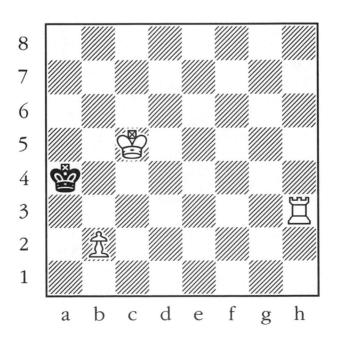

91.

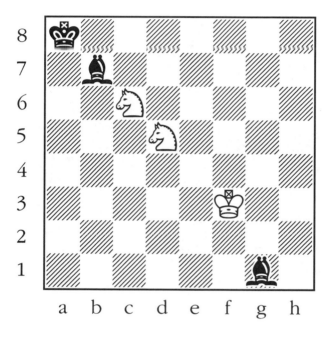

92.

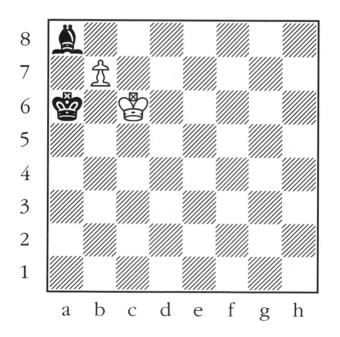

93.

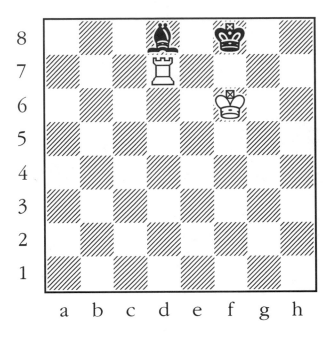

94.

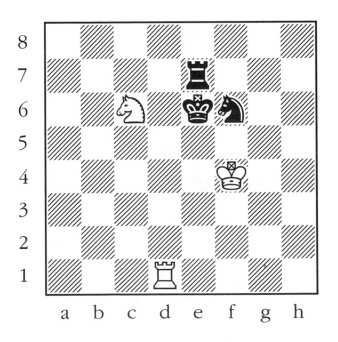

95.

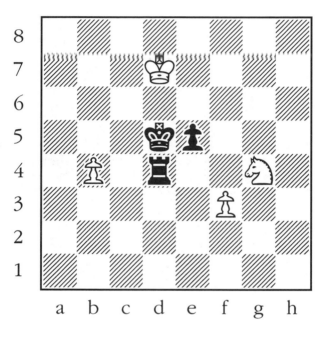

96.

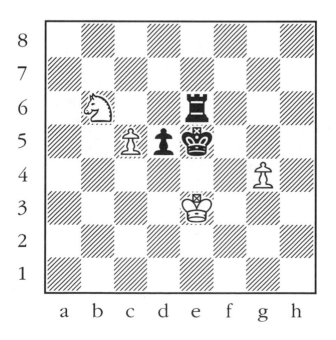

97.

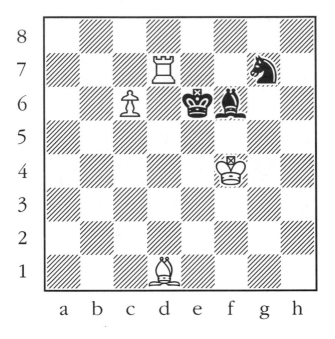

98.

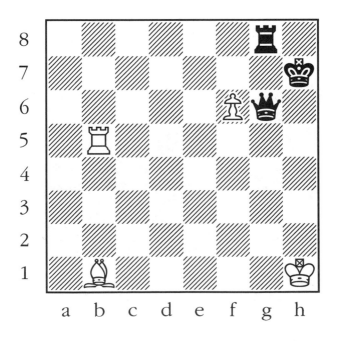

99.

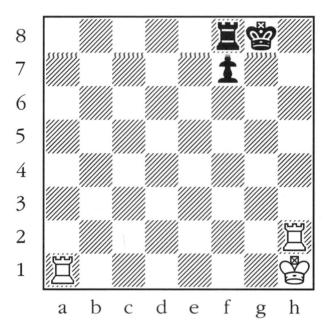

100.

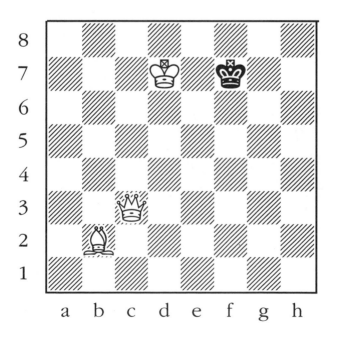

CHECKMATE IN TWO MOVES

Now it's time to try something a bit more tricky. These next 102 positions, diagram numbers 101-202, are White to checkmate in **two** moves. Now there are two moves to think about, instead of one like in the earlier diagrams. Work hard on these diagrams, and try not to look at the answers in the back until after you've tried them all a couple times.

101.

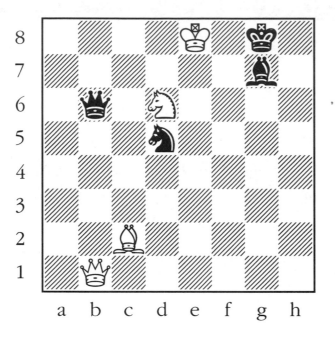

102.

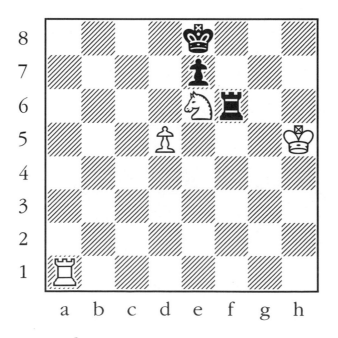

103.

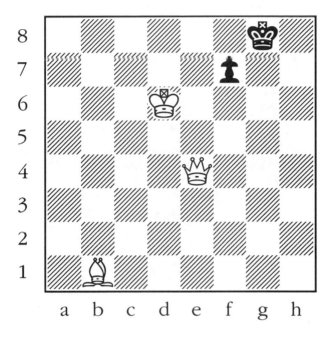

104.

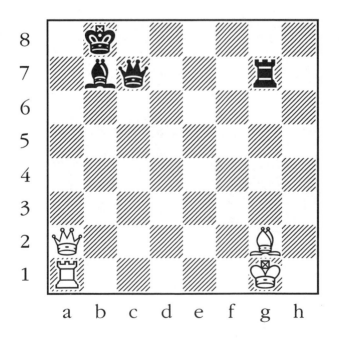

105.

106.

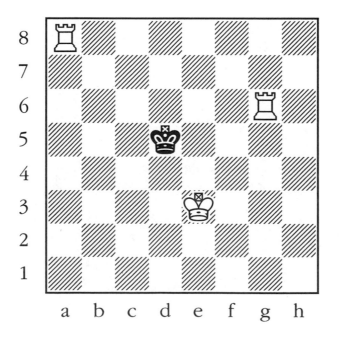

107.

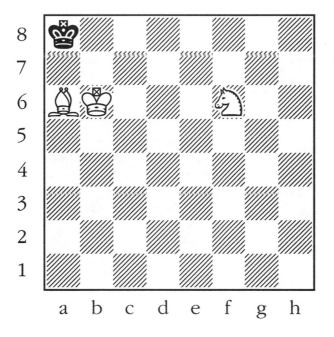

108.

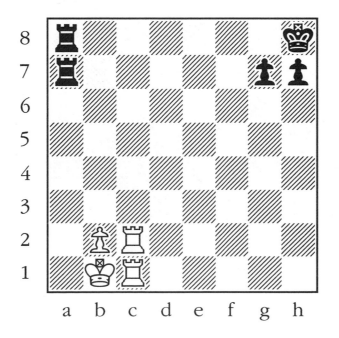

109.

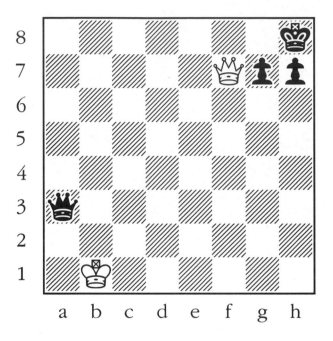

110.

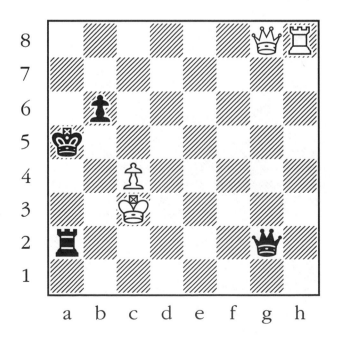

111.

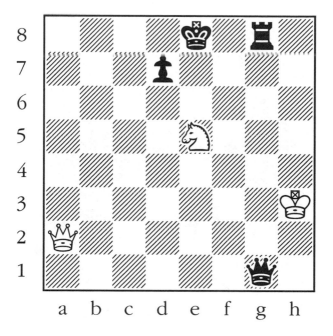

112.

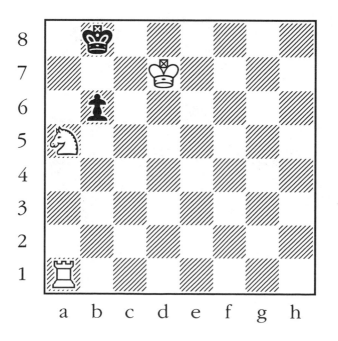

113.

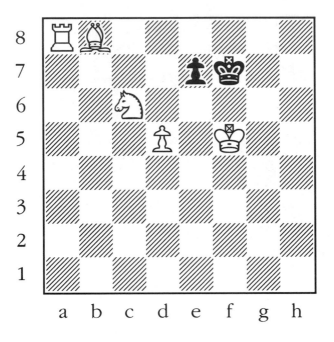

114.

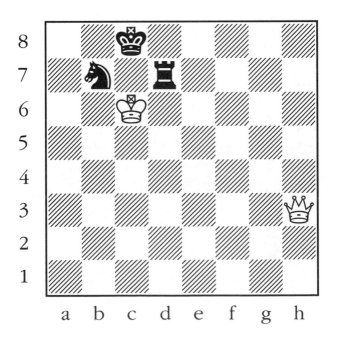

115.

116.

117.

118.

119.

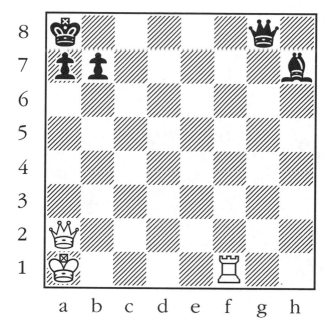

120.

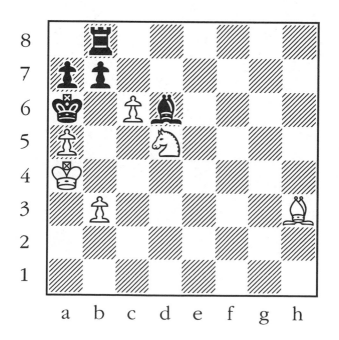

121.

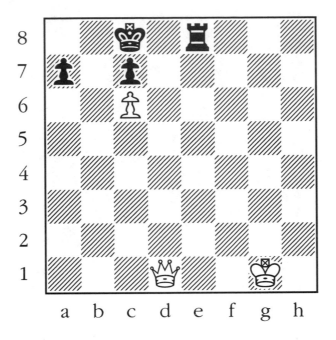

122.

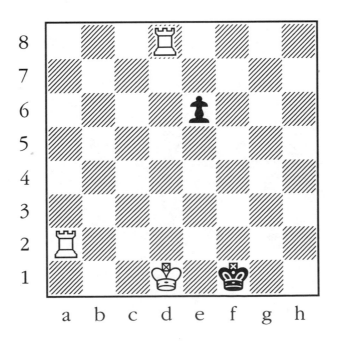

123.

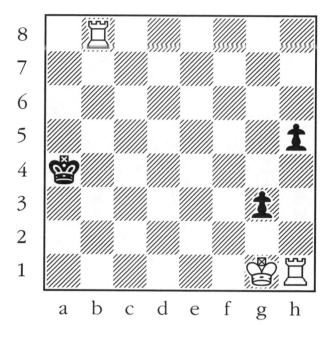

124.

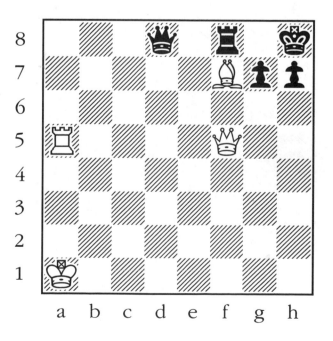

125.

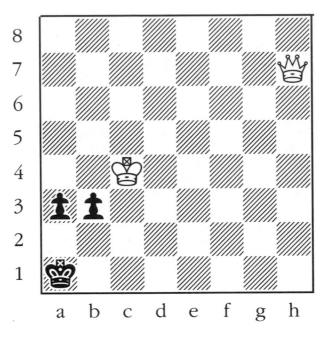

126.

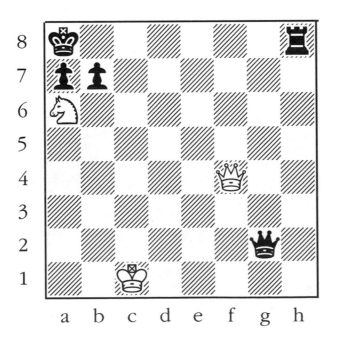

127.

128.

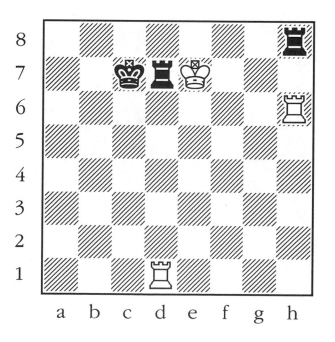

129.

130.

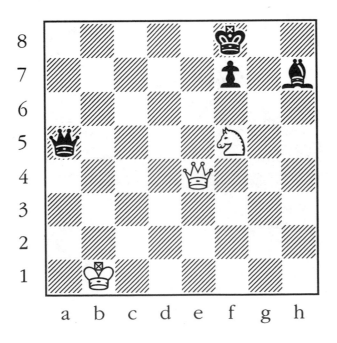

131.

132.

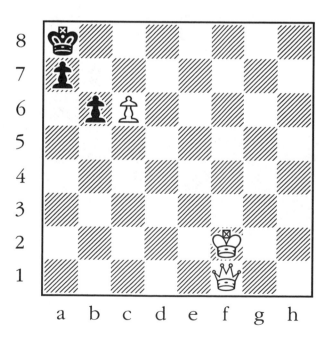

133.

134.

135.

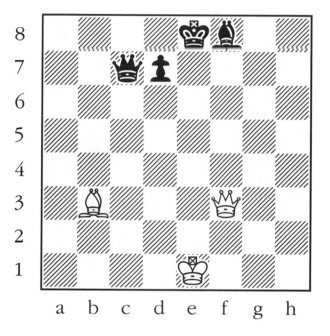

136.

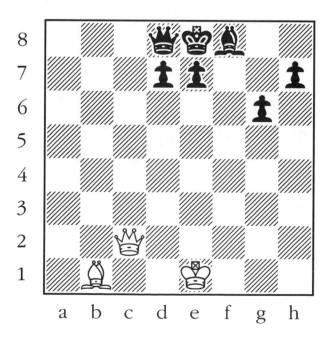

137.

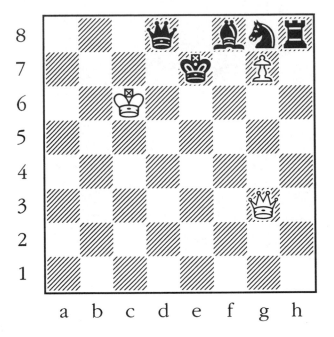

138.

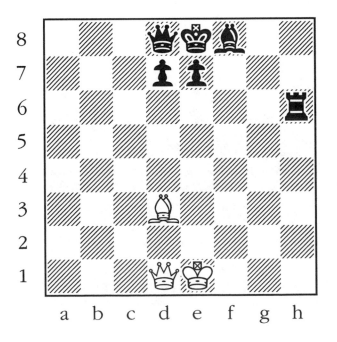

139.

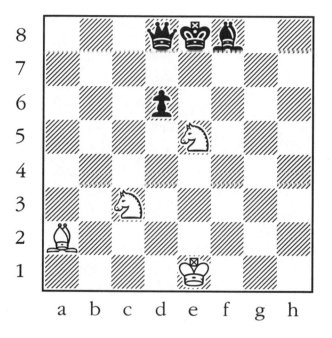

140.

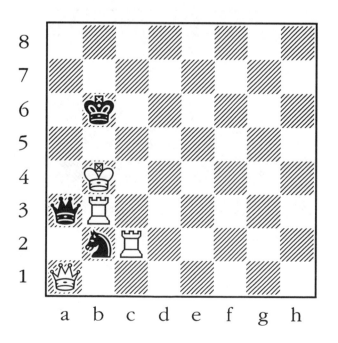

141.

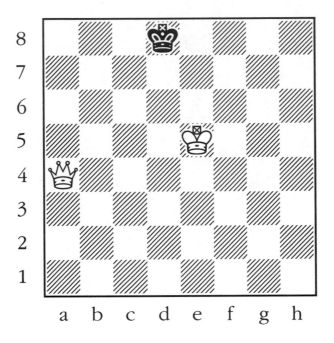

142.

143.

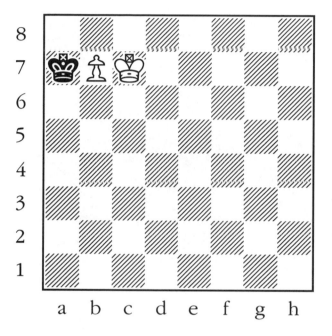

144.

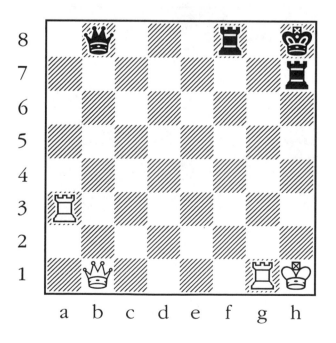

145.

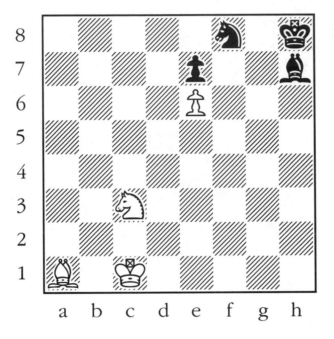

146.

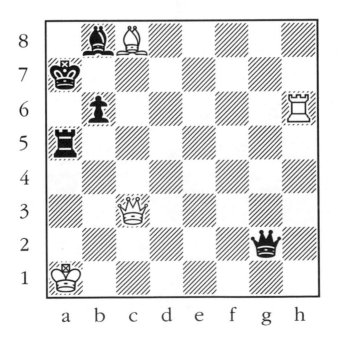

147.

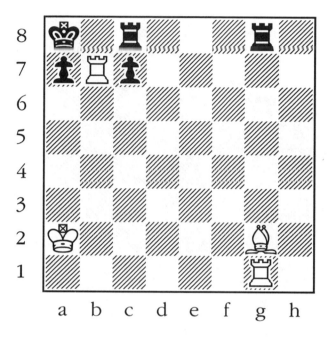

148.

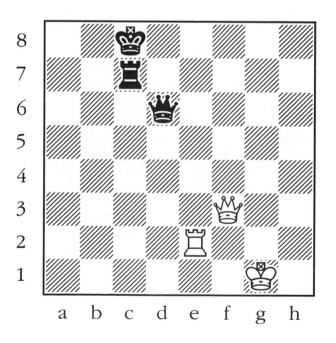

149.

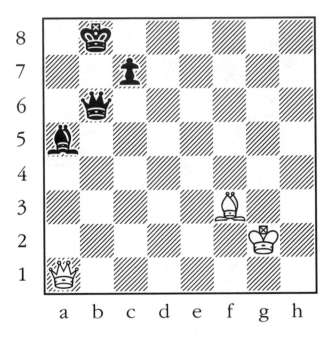

150.

151.

152.

153.

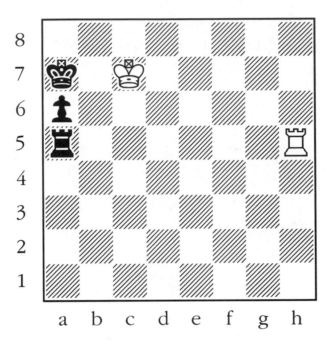

154.

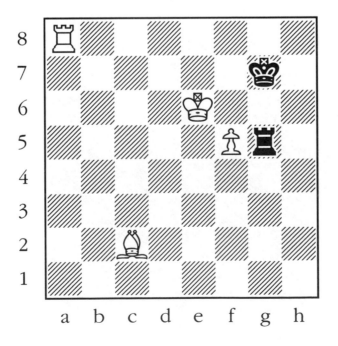

155.

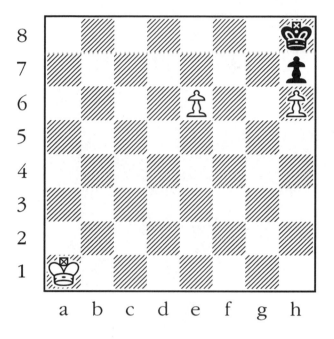

156.

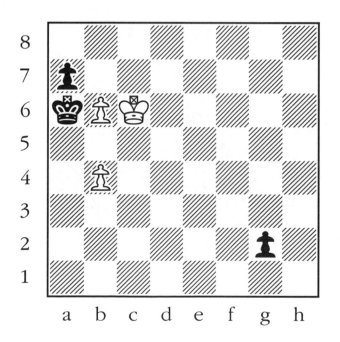

157.

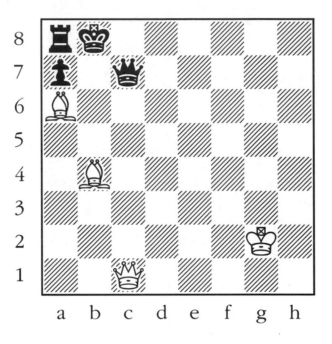

158.

159.

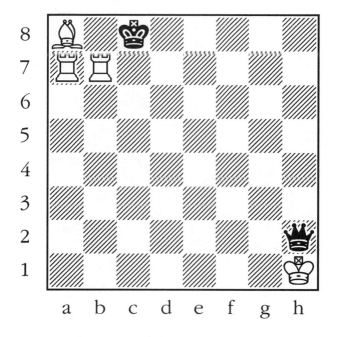

160.

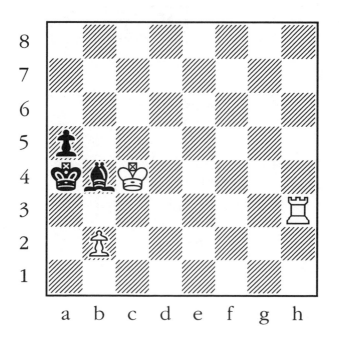

161.

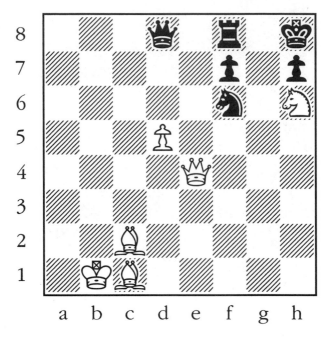

162.

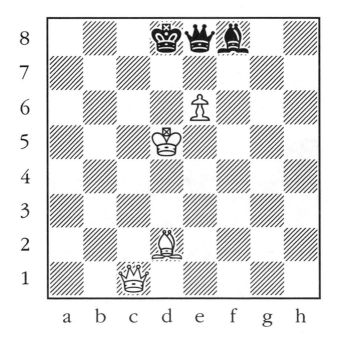

163.

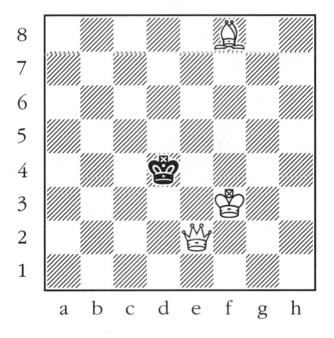

164.

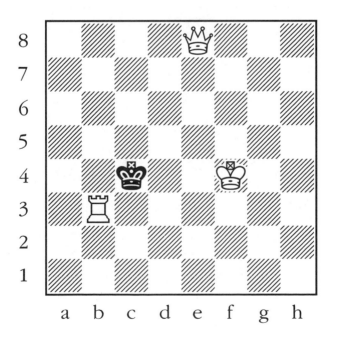

165.

166.

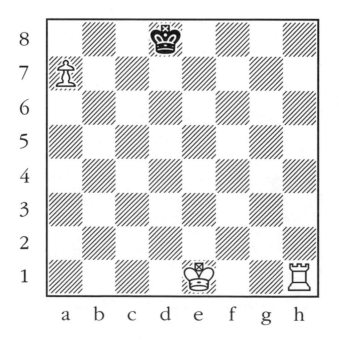

167.

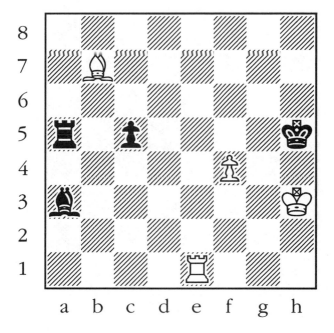

168.

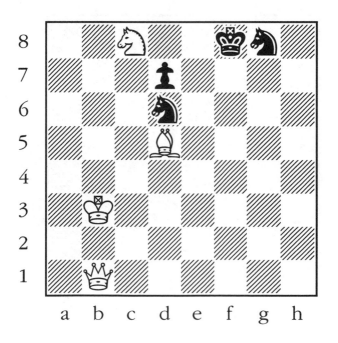

169.

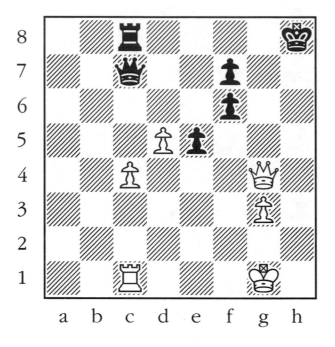

170.

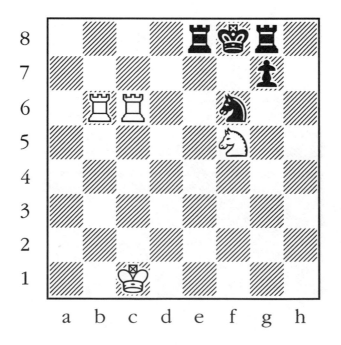

171.

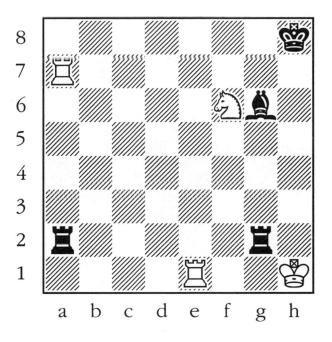

172.

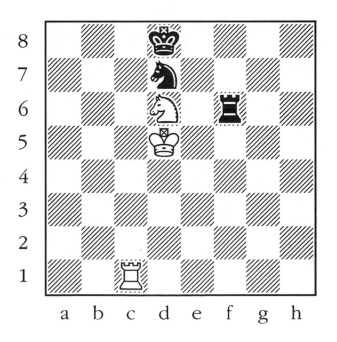

173.

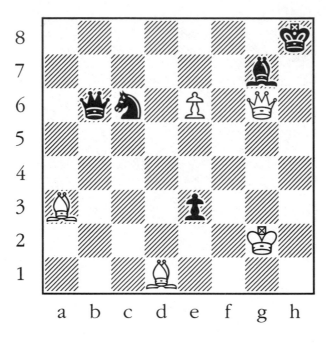

174.

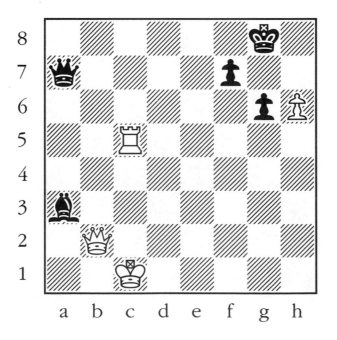

175.

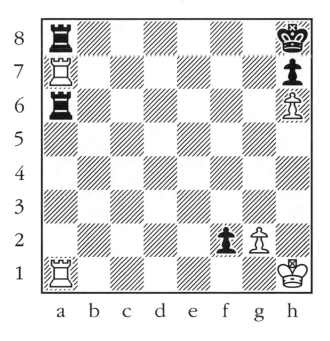

176.

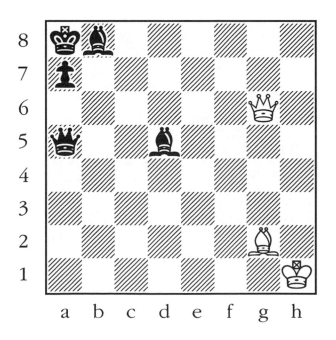

177.

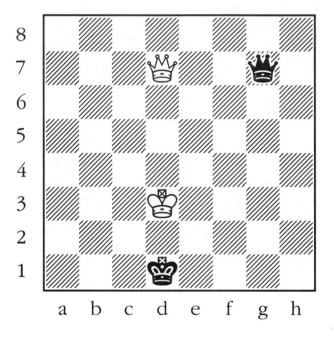

178.

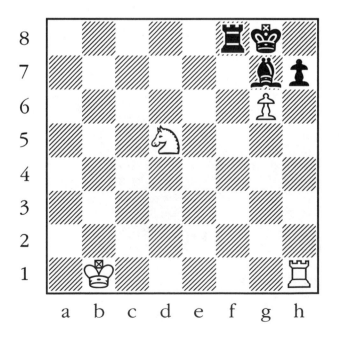

179.

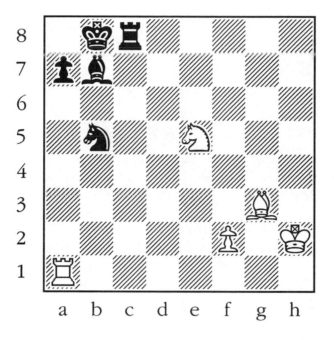

180.

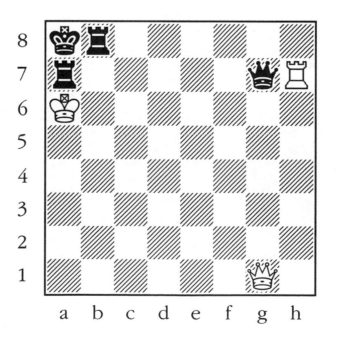

181.

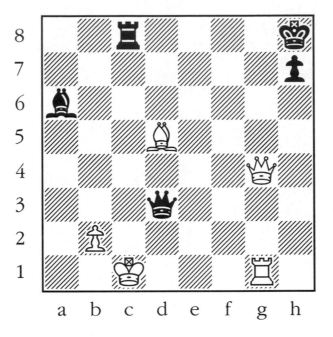

182.

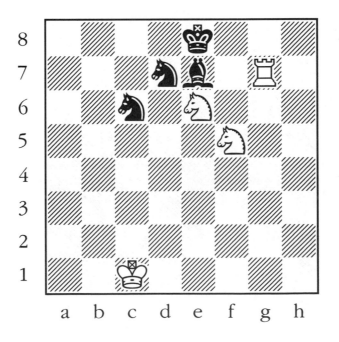

183.

184.

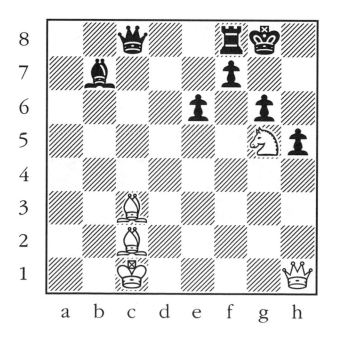

185.

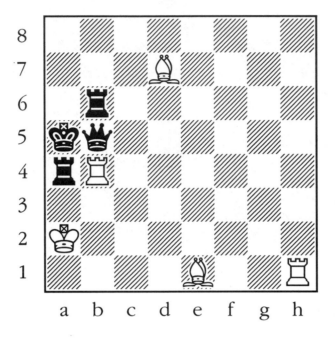

186.

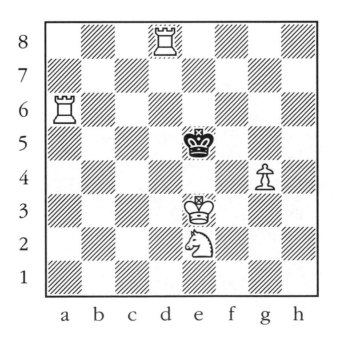

187.

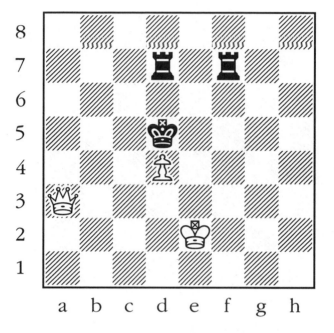

188.

189.

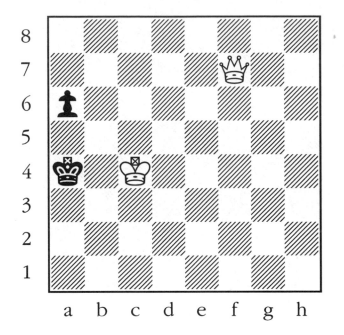

190.

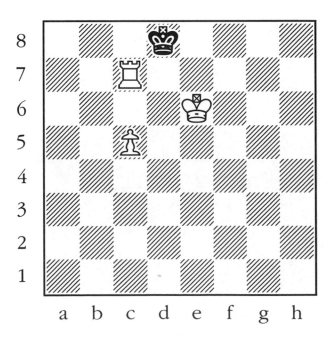

191.

192.

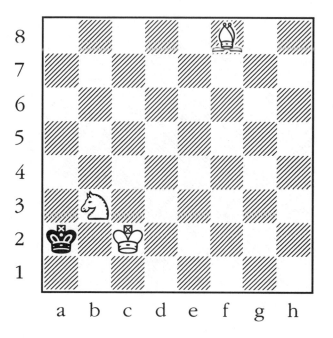

193.

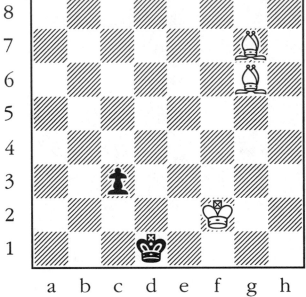

194.

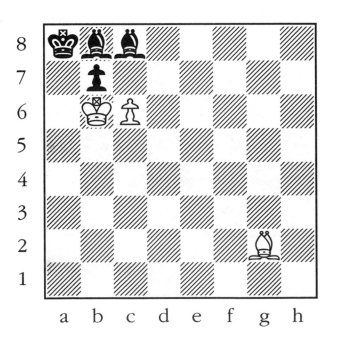

195.

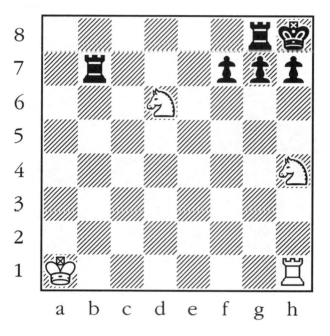

196.

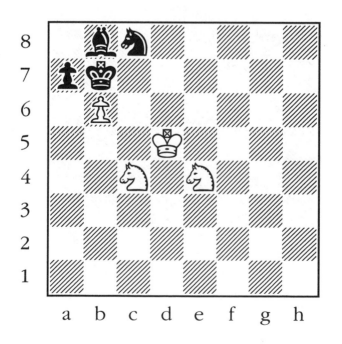

197.

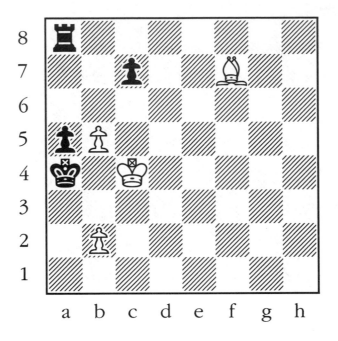

198.

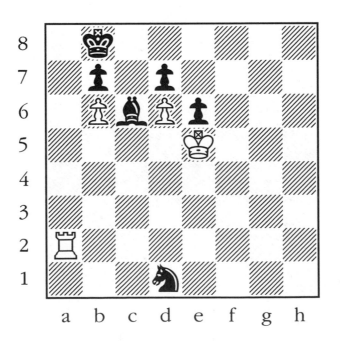

199.

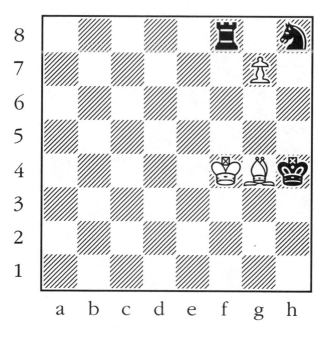

200.

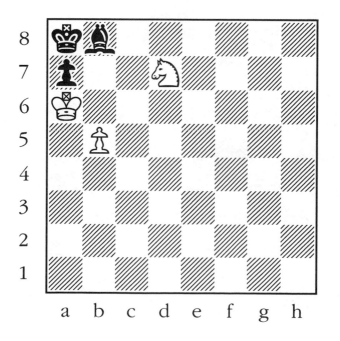

201.

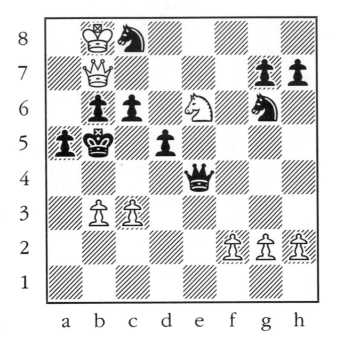

202.

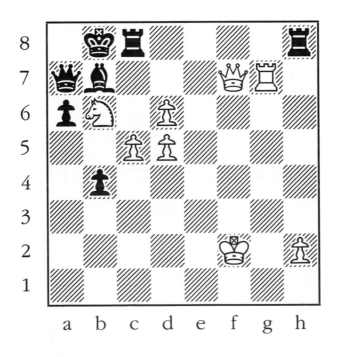

Wow! Those last two positions were very tough! We hope you were able to solve them, but if not, don't stop trying yet. How about a hint?

Look for a possible "big sacrifice," like the kind we talked about in the introduction. Remember that you can give up even your strongest piece to force checkmate. We are sure you will find the solutions now!

Okay, now that you have finished going through your first chess workbook what should you do? Well, besides getting some more chess books to study, keep practicing solving the mates in our book until they are all easy to find. Remember, practice makes perfect!

THE SOLUTIONS

LIST OF SOLUTIONS

Have you tried all the checkmates? They can be tricky, but keep trying until you feel confident with each one.

If you've done them all and you're ready to check your work, then look through the following pages for the answers.

Remember to give each checkmate a good try before looking at the solutions, and good luck!

DIAGRAM OF SOLUTIONS

#1 1.Ra8 mate

#4 1.Qh7 mate

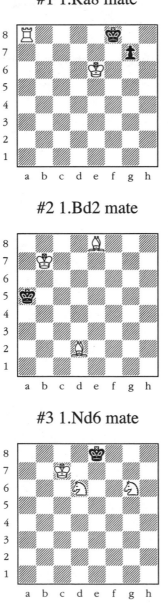

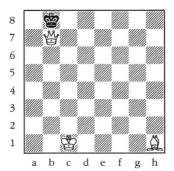

#2 1.Bd2 mate

#5 1.Qb7 mate

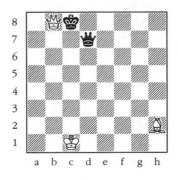

#3 1.Nd6 mate

#6 1.Qb8 mate

DIAGRAM OF SOLUTIONS

#7 1.Qg8 mate

#11 1.Qc6 mate

#8 1.Qd4 mate

#12 1.Qg6 mate

#9 1.Ne2 mate

#13 1.f7 mate

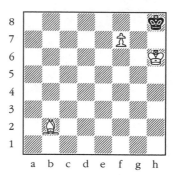

#10 1.Rc8 mate

#14 1.Kb3 mate

#15 1.Rf6 mate

#19 1.Be6 mate

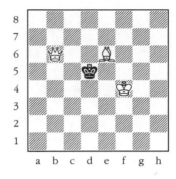

#16 1.Ra7 mate

#20 1.Qf7 mate

#17 1.Nd6 mate

#21 1.Qc2 mate

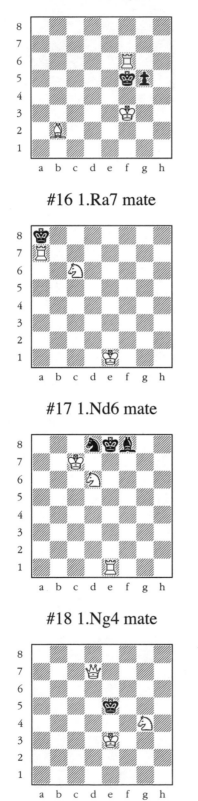

#18 1.Ng4 mate

#22 1.Qg7 mate

DIAGRAM OF SOLUTIONS

#23 1.b4 mate

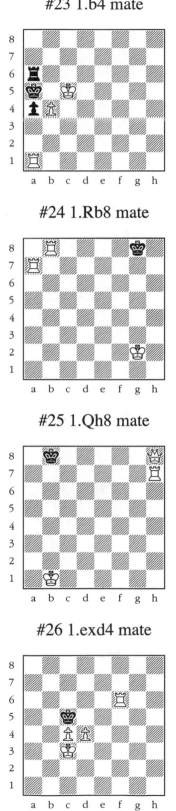

#27 1.e7 mate

#24 1.Rb8 mate

#28 1.g4 mate

#25 1.Qh8 mate

#29 1.d8/N mate

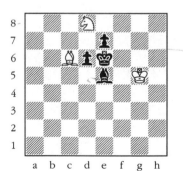

#26 1.exd4 mate

#30 1.Ne6 mate

#31 1.Ba6 mate

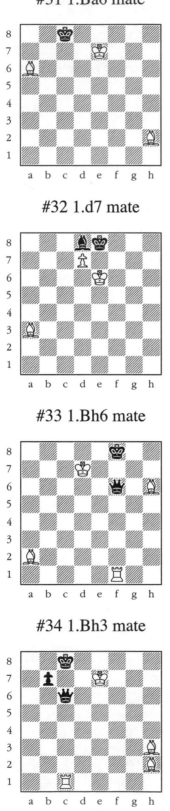

#35 1.Rh8 mate

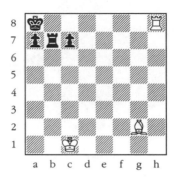

#32 1.d7 mate

#36 1.Be5 mate

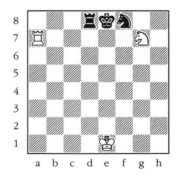

#33 1.Bh6 mate

#37 1.Ng7 mate

#34 1.Bh3 mate

#38 1.Bg7 mate

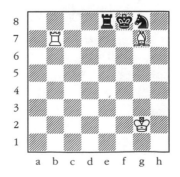

DIAGRAM OF SOLUTIONS

#39 1.b3 mate

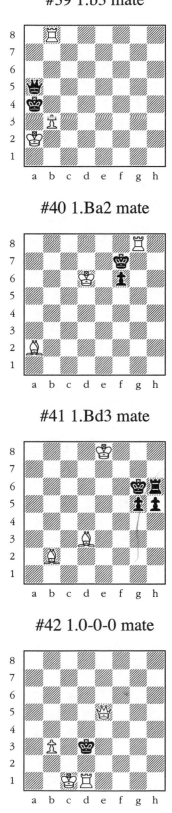

#43 1.Qa7 mate

#40 1.Ba2 mate

#44 1.c7 mate

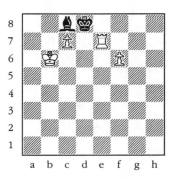

#41 1.Bd3 mate

#45 1.Nc4 mate

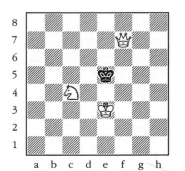

#42 1.0-0-0 mate

#46 1.Qh4 mate

#47 1.Ra1 mate

#51 1.Ne4 mate

#48 1.c4 mate

#52 1.Ng3 mate

#49 1.Qd5 mate

#53 1.Nf7 mate

#50 1.Qc6 mate

#54 1.b7 mate

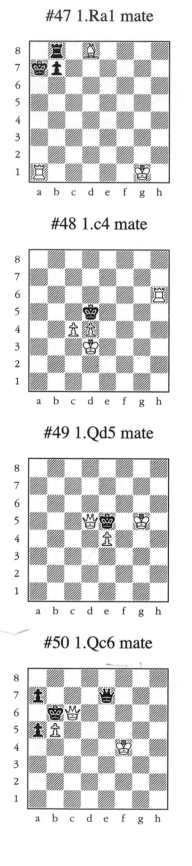

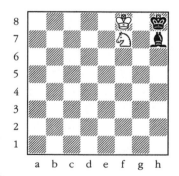
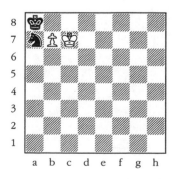

DIAGRAM OF SOLUTIONS

#55 1.b8/Q mate

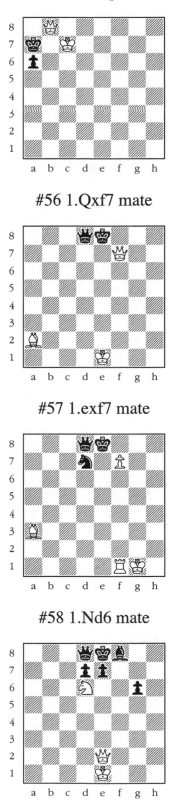

#59 1.Bf7 mate

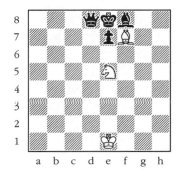

#56 1.Qxf7 mate

#60 1.Nf6 mate

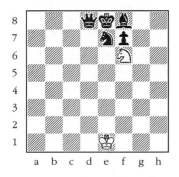

#57 1.exf7 mate

#61 1.Qc8 mate

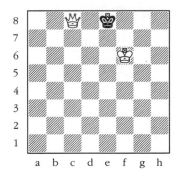

#58 1.Nd6 mate

#62 1.Qa8 mate

#63 1.Qc8 mate

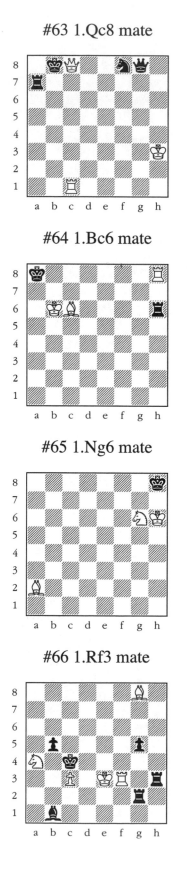

#64 1.Bc6 mate

#65 1.Ng6 mate

#66 1.Rf3 mate

#67 1.Bg1 mate

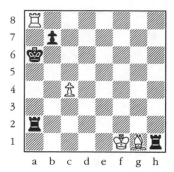

#68 1.Qxe4 mate

#69 1.Rxb2 mate

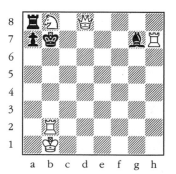

#70 1.Rh8 mate

DIAGRAM OF SOLUTIONS

#71 1.Qc7 mate

#75 1.Ke3 mate

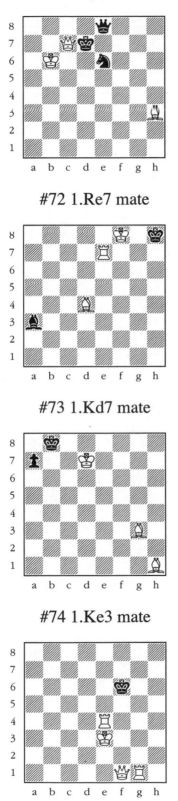

#72 1.Re7 mate

#76 1.Rg8 mate

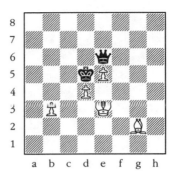

#73 1.Kd7 mate

#77 1.Qxe7 mate

#74 1.Ke3 mate

#78 1.Nh6 mate

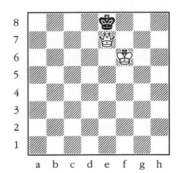

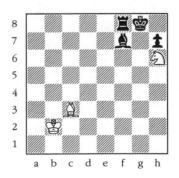

#79 1.Rh2 mate

#83 1.Qa3 mate

#80 1.Nd7 mate

#84 1.cxb3 mate

#81 1.Rc6 mate

#85 1.Bxg7 mate

#82 1.Qa8 mate

#86 1.Rc8 mate

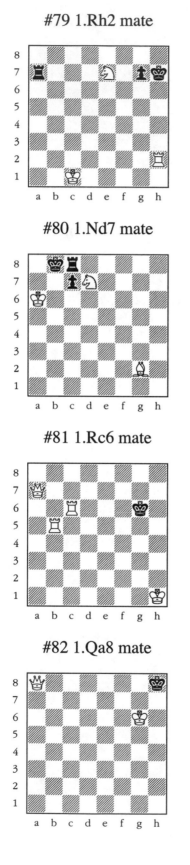
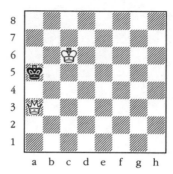

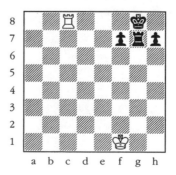

DIAGRAM OF SOLUTIONS

#87 1.Rh1 mate

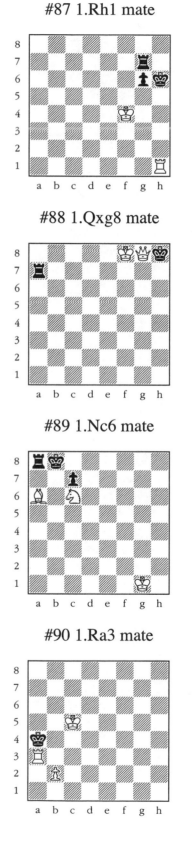

#91 1.Nc7 mate

#88 1.Qxg8 mate

#92 1.bxa8/Q mate

#89 1.Nc6 mate

#93 1.Rxd8 mate

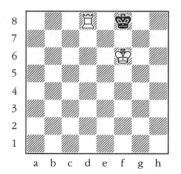

#90 1.Ra3 mate

#94 1.Nd8 mate

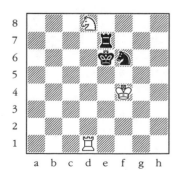

#95 1.Ne3 mate

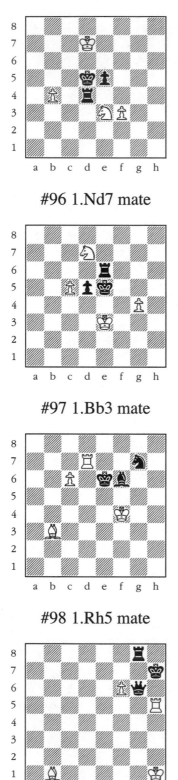

#96 1.Nd7 mate

#97 1.Bb3 mate

#98 1.Rh5 mate

#99 1.Rg1 mate

#100 1.Qg7 mate

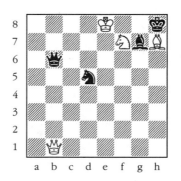

#101 1.Bh7+ Kh8 2.Nf7#

#102 1.Ra8+ Kf7 (or 1...Kd7 2.Rd8#) 2.Rf8#

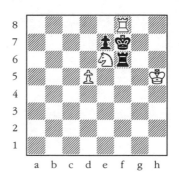

#103 1.Qh7+ Kf8 2.Qh8#

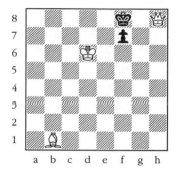

#107 1.Bb7+ Kb8 2.Nd7#

#104 1.Qa8+ Bxa8 2.Rxa8#

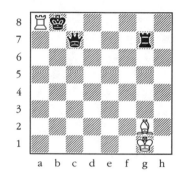

#108 1.Rc8+ Rxc8 2.Rxc8#

#105 1.Kc4 Ka5 2.Qa7#

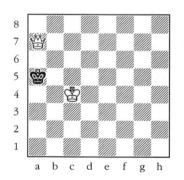

#109 1.Qe8+ Qf8 2.Qxf8#

#106 1.Rc8 Ke5 2.Rc5#

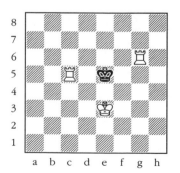

#110 1.Qa8+ Qxa8 2.Rxa8#

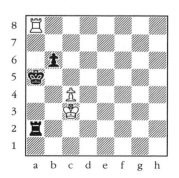

#111 1.Qf7+ Kd8 2.Qxd7#

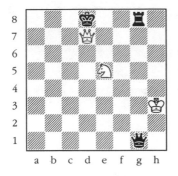

#115 1.Rxf6 Kh8 2.Rf8#

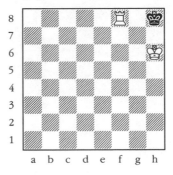

#112 1.Nc6+ Kb7 2.Ra7#

#116 1.b8/R Kh2 2.Rh8# Not 1.b8/Q? stalemate

#113 1.Be5 e6 2.dxe6#

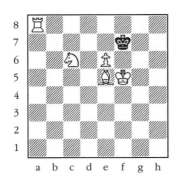

#117 1.Ra8 Kh6 2.Rh8#

#114 1.Qxd7+ Kb8 2.Qxb7#

#118 1.Bd5+ Kh8 2.Rf8#

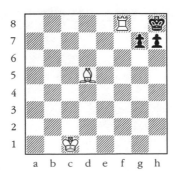

DIAGRAM OF SOLUTIONS

#119 1.Qxg8+ Bxg8 2.Rf8#

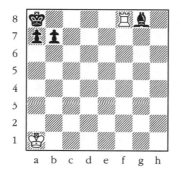

#123 1.Kg2 Ka3 (or any other move) 2.Ra1#

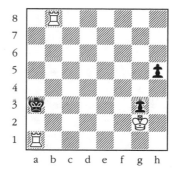

#120 1.Bf1+ b5 2.axb5e.p.#

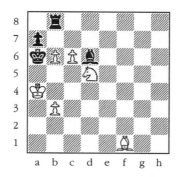

#124 1.Qxh7+ Kxh7 2.Rh5#

#121 1.Qd7+ Kb8 2.Qxe8#

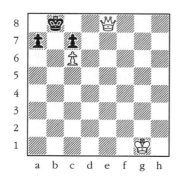

#125 1.Kxb3 a2 2.Qh1#

#122 1.Kc1 Ke1 (or any other move) 2.Rd1#

#126 1.Qb8+ Rxb8 2.Nc7#

#127 1.Ng4 h2 2.Nf2#

#131 1.Rg8+ Rxg8 2.Nf7#

#128 1.Rxd7+ Kc8 2.Rxh8#

#132 1.Qa6 Kb8 (or any other move) 2.Qb7#

#129 1.Nf6+ Nxf6 2.Nxf6#

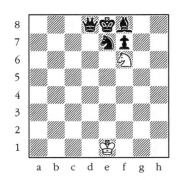

#133 1.Rb8 Kxh6 2.Rh8#

#130 1.Qe7+ Kg8 2.Qe8#

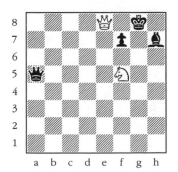

#134 1.Qg4 Ka6 2.Qa4#

#135 1.Qf7+ Kd8 2.Qxf8#

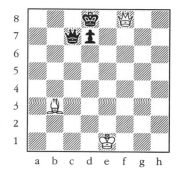

#136 1.Qxg6+ hxg6 2.Bxg6#

#137 1.Qe5+ Kf7 2.gxh8/N#

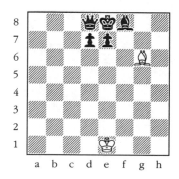

#138 1.Qh5+ Rxh5 (or 1...Rg6 2.Q[B]xg6#) 2.Bg6#

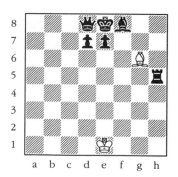

#139 1.Bf7+ Ke7 2.Nd5#

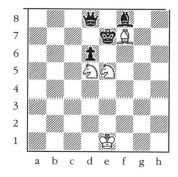

#140 1.Kxa3+ Ka5 2.Kxb2#

#141 1.Kd6 Kc8 2.Qa8#

#142 1.Rc8 Ke1 2.Rc1#

#143 1.b8/Q+ Ka6 2.Qb6#

#147 1.Rb8+ Kxb8 2.Rb1#

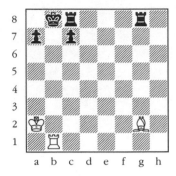

#144 1.Qxh7+ Kxh7 2.Rh3#

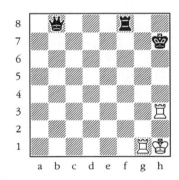

#148 1.Qa8+ Kd7 2.Qe8#

#145 1.Nd5+ Kg8 2.Nxe7#

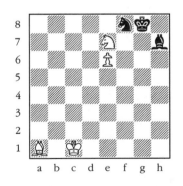

#149 1.Qh8+ Ka7 2.Qa8#

#146 1.Qxa5+ bxa5 2.Ra6#

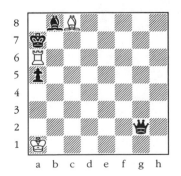

#150 1.Ba2+ Kh8 2.Bb2#

#151 1.f7+ Kf8 2.Ba3#

#155 1.e7 Kg8 2.e8/Q#

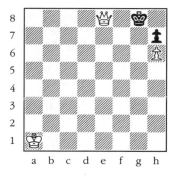

#152 1.cxb7+ Kb8 2.Nc6#

#156 1.b7 g1/Q 2.b8/N#

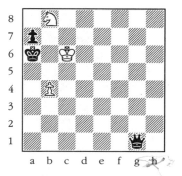

#153 1.Rxa5 Ka8 2.Rxa6#

#157 1.Bd6 Qxd6 2.Qc8#

#154 1.f6+ Kh6 2.Rh8#

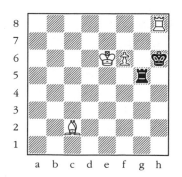

#158 1.Rb7 Ke8 2.Rg8#

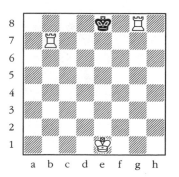

#159 1.Kxh2 Kd8 2.Rb8#

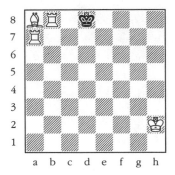

#163 1.Bb4 Kd5 2.Qe4#

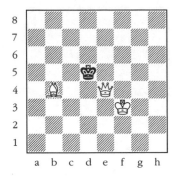

#160 1.Ra3+ Bxa3 2.b3#

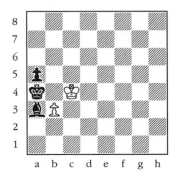

#164 1.Qb5+ Kd4 2.Rd3#

#161 1.Bb2 Kg7 (or any other move) 2.Qxh7#

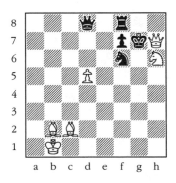

#165 1.Qe6+ Kd8 2.Rc8#

#162 1.Ba5+ Ke7 2.Qg5#

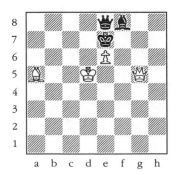

#166 1.Rh7 Kc8 2.a8/Q#

DIAGRAM OF SOLUTIONS

#167 1.Re6 Bb4 (or any other move) 2.Bf3#

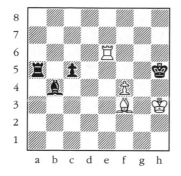

#171 1.Re8+ Bxe8 2.Rh7#

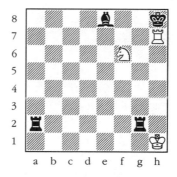

#168 1.Qh7 Ke8 2.Qxg8# If Nf6 2 Qe7#; if Nxc8 2.Qf7#

#172 1. Rc8+ Ke7 2.Re8#

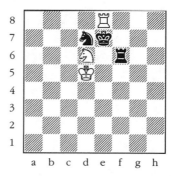

#169 1.Kg2 Rg8 (or any other move) 2.Rh1#

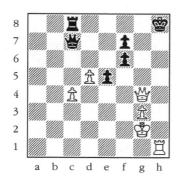

#173 1.Bc2 Kg8 2.Qh7#

#170 1.Rxf6+ gxf6 2.Rxf6#

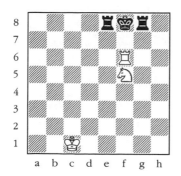

#174 1.Rc8+ Kh7 (1...Bf8 2.Qg7#) 2.Rh8#

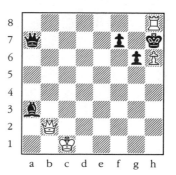

#175 1.Rxa8+ Rxa8 2.Rxa8#

#179 1.Nd7+ Ka8 2.Nb6#

#176 1.Qc6+ Bxc6 2.Bxc6#

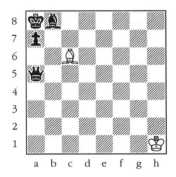

#180 1.Qxa7+ Qxa7 2.Rxa7#

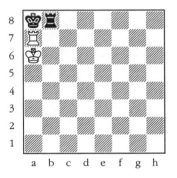

#177 1.Qxg7 Ke1 (1...Kc1 2.Qa1#) 2.Qg1#

#181 1.Qxc8+ Bxc8 2.Rg8#

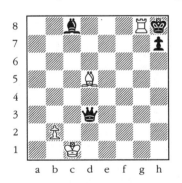

#178 1.Ne7+ Kh8 2.Rxh7#

#182 1.Rxe7+ Nxe7 2.Nd6#

#183 1.Nc6+ Ka6[a8] 2.Qa7#

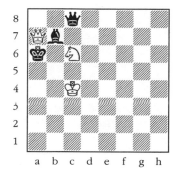

#187 1.Qc5+ Ke4 2.Qe5#

#184 1.Qxh5 gxh5 (or else Qh7[h8]#) 2.Bh7#

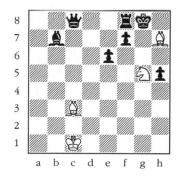

#188 1.Kd3 Kc5 2.Ne4#

#185 1.Rxa4+ Kxa4 2.Rh4#

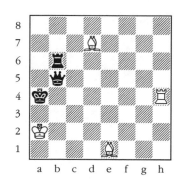

#189 1.Qb7 Ka5 2.Qb4# If 1...Ka3[Pa5] 2.Qb3#

#186 1.Kf2 Ke4 2.Re6#

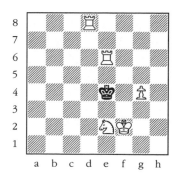

#190 1.Rc6 Ke8 2.Rc8#

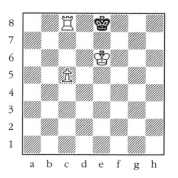

#191 1.Nc1+ Ka1 2.Bg7#

#195 1.Nxf7+ Rxf7 2.Ng6#

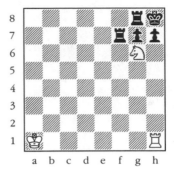

#192 1.Bg2+ Kh2 2.Ng4#

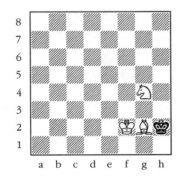

#196 1.Nc5+ Ka8 2.b7#

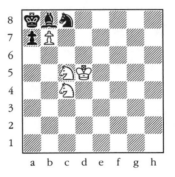

#193 1.Bh6 c2 2.Bh5#

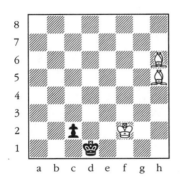

#197 1.Bg6 Rg8 (or any other move) 2.Bc2#

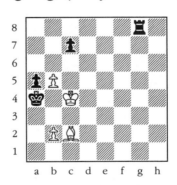

#194 1.cxb7+ Bxb7 2.Bxb7#

#198 1.Rh2 Ne3 (or any other move) 2.Rh8#

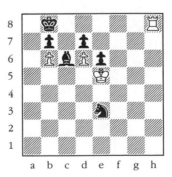

158

DIAGRAM OF SOLUTIONS

#199 1.gxf8/N Nf7 2.Ng6#

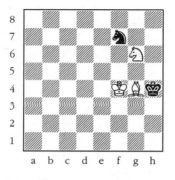

#200 1.b6 axb6 (or bishop moves 2.b7#) 2.Nxb6#

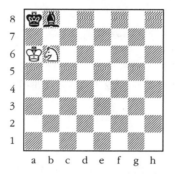

#201 1.Qa6+ Kxa6 2.Nc7#

#202 1.Qc7+ Rxc7 2.dxc7#

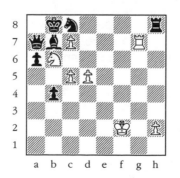

GREAT CARDOZA CHESS BOOKS
ADD THESE TO YOUR LIBRARY · ORDER NOW!

303 TRICKY CHECKMATES by Fred Wilson & Bruce Alberston. Both a fascinating challenge and great training tool, these two, three and four move checkmates are great for beginning, intermediate and expert players. Mates are in order of difficulty, from simple to very complex positions. Learn the standard patterns for cornering the king, corridor and support mates, attraction and deflection sacrifices, pins and annihilation, the quiet move, and the dreaded zugzwang. Examples from old classics to the 1990's illustrate a wide range of ideas. 192 pgs. $12.95.

303 TRICKY CHESS TACTICS by Fred Wilson & Bruce Alberston. This is not just a challenging collection of two and three move tactical surprises for the advanced beginner, intermediate, and expert player—it's also a great training tool! Tactics are presented in order of difficulty so that players can advance from the simple to the complex positions. The examples, from actual games, illustrate a wide range of chess tactics from old classics right up to today. Great stuff! 192 pgs. $12.95.

ENCYCLOPEDIA OF CHESS WISDOM by Eric Schiller. The most important concepts, strategies, tactics, wisdom, and thinking that every chessplayer must know, plus the gold nuggets of knowledge behind every attack and defense, is collected together in one volume. From opening, middlegame, and endgame strategy, to psychological warfare and tournament tactics, the reader is taken through the thinking behind each essential concept. Through examples, discussions, and diagrams, you are shown the full impact on the game's direction. 432 pgs. $19.95

CHESS ENDGAME QUIZ by Larry Evans. This book features 200 challenges in the multiple choice format. These instructive, elegant and entertaining positions will not only challenge and entertain you but teach you how to improve your engame while trying to find the best move of the three choices presented. Sections include king and pawn endings, minor piece endings, queen endings, rook and pawn endings so you can concentrate on specific areas. What is the best move? Take the plunge and find out! 304 pgs. $14.95

THE 10 MOST COMMON CHESS MISTAKES...AND HOW TO FIX THEM by Larry Evans. A fascinating collection of more than 200 typical errors committed by the world's greatest players challenges readers to test their skills by choosing between two moves, the right one, or the one actually played. Readers will be amazed at how even world champions stumble by violating basic principles. From neglecting development, king safety, misjudging threats, premature attacks, to impulsiveness, snatching pawns, and basic inattention, readers get a complete course in exactly where they can go wrong and how to fix their game. 256 pgs. $14.95.

WINNING CHESS OPENINGS by Bill Robertie. Shows the concepts, moves and best opening moves from Black's and White's perspectives of more than 25 essential openings: King's Gambit, Center Game, Scotch Game, Giucco Piano, Vienna Game, Bishop's Opening, Ruy Lopez, French, Caro-Kann, Sicilian, Alekhine, Pirc, Modern, Queen's Gambit, Nimzo-Indian, Queen's Indian, Dutch, King's Indian, Benoni, English, Bird's, Reti's, and King's Indian Attack. Includes actual examples from 25 grandmasters and champions including Fischer, Kasparov and Spassky. 176 pgs. $9.95